# People in the Community

# Vets

## Diyan Leake

**Heinemann**
LIBRARY

**www.heinemann.co.uk/library**
Visit our website to find out more information about Heinemann Library books.

To order:
☎ Phone 44 (0) 1865 888066
📄 Send a fax to 44 (0) 1865 314091
💻 Visit the Heinemann Bookshop at www.heinemann.co.uk/library to browse our catalogue and order online.

First published in Great Britain by Heinemann Library, Halley Court, Jordan Hill, Oxford OX2 8EJ, part of Pearson Education.
Heinemann is a registered trademark of Pearson Education Ltd.

Editorial: Diyan Leake and Catherine Clarke
Design: Joanna Hinton-Malivoire and Steve Mead
Picture research: Tracy Cummins and Heather Maudlin
Production: Alison Parsons

Origination: Chroma Graphics (Overseas) Pte Ltd
Printed and bound in China by South China Printing Company Ltd

ISBN 978 0 431 19247 5
12 11 10 09 08
10 9 8 7 6 5 4 3 2 1

**British Library Cataloguing in Publication Data**
Leake, Diyan
Vets. - (People in the community)
636'.089
A full catalogue record for this book is available from the British Library.

**Acknowledgments**
The publishers would like to thank the following for permission to reproduce photographs:
©Alamy pp. **13** (Jim Wileman), **14** (Arco Images), **21** (Blend Images); ©Associated Press pp. **6** (Jessie Cohen), **10**, **17** (Steve Chernek), **22 (bottom)** (Steve Cherneck); ©Corbis pp. **15** (Larry Williams/Zefa), **19** (Jim Craigmyle), **20** (Frank Lukasseck); ©digitalrailroad (Stewart Cohen) pp. **8**, **22 (middle)**; ©Getty Images pp. **4** (Ingolf Pompe), **7** (Gary Benson), **9** (Li Zhong/ChinaFotoPress), **18** (Hassan Ammar/AFP), **22 (top)** (Ingolf Pompe); ©Peter Arnold Inc. pp. **11** (PHONE Labat J.M./Rouquette F.), **12** (PHONE Labat J.M./Rouquette F.), **16** (Jorgen Schytte); ©Shutterstock (Emin Kuliyev) p. **5**.

Front cover photograph of a vet examining a chimpanzee on Ngamba Island reproduced with permission of ©Corbis (Penny Tweedie). Back cover photograph reproduced with permission of ©Alamy (Blend Images).

Every effort has been made to contact copyright holders of any material reproduced in this book. Any omissions will be rectified in subsequent printings if notice is given to the publisher.

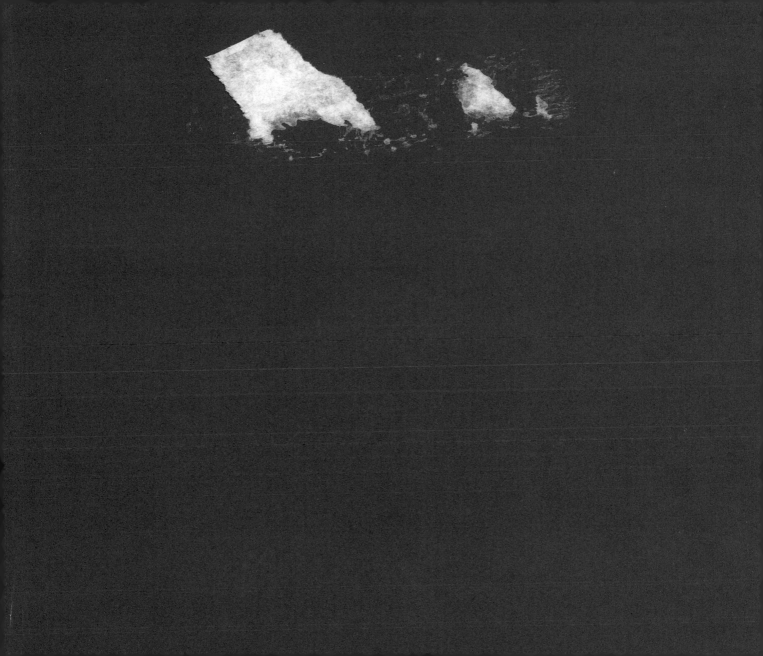

# Contents

# Communities

People live in communities. They live near each other and help each other.

People work together in a community.

# Vets in the community

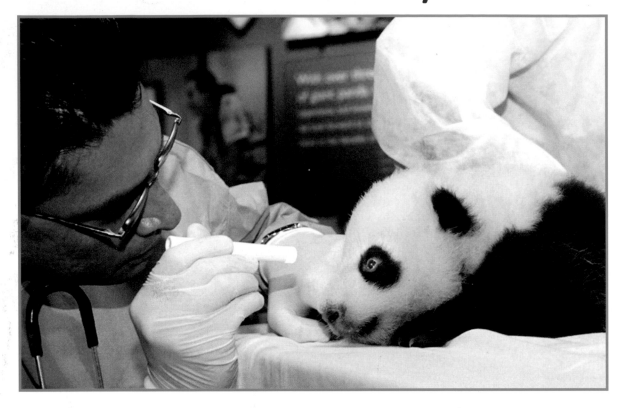

Vets work in communities.

Vets help animals stay healthy.

# What vets do

Vets help pets stay healthy.

Vets help wild animals stay healthy.

Vets help animals when they are sick.

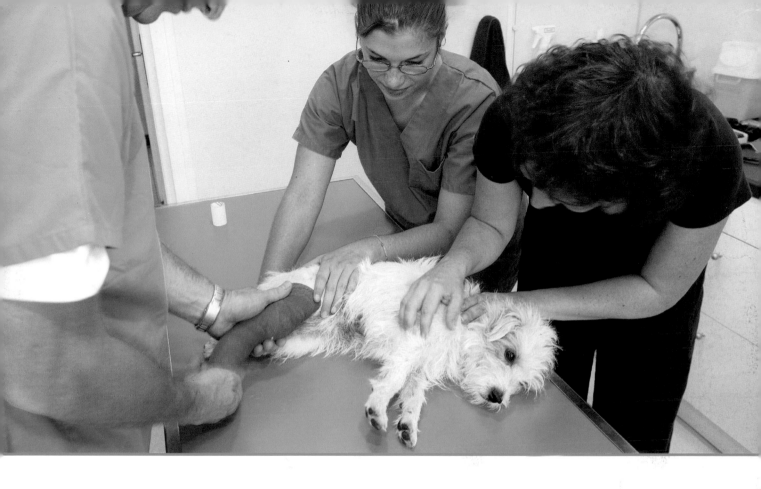

Vets help animals when they are hurt.

# Where vets work

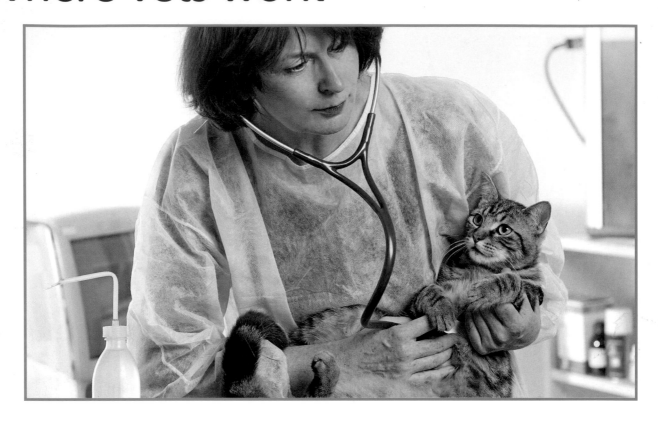

Vets work in clinics.

Vets work on farms.

# What vets use

Vets use special equipment.

Vets use their hands.

# People who work with vets

Vets work with farmers.

Vets work with zookeepers.

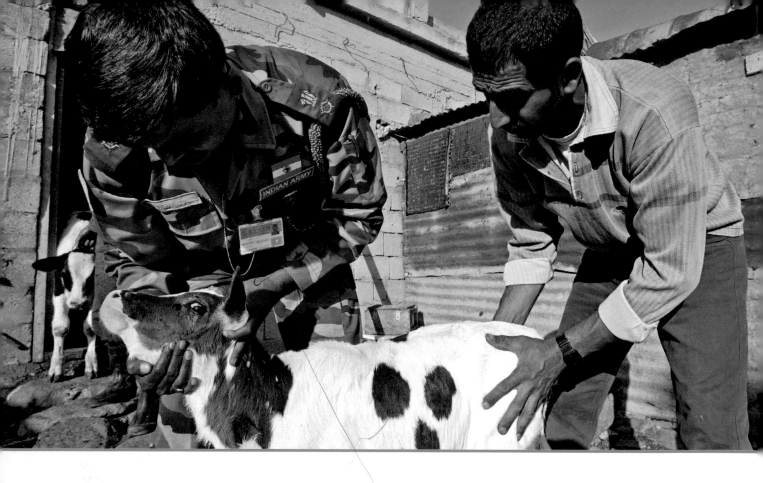

Vets work with adults who have sick animals.

Vets work with children who have
sick pets.

# How vets help us

Vets help animals stay healthy.

Vets help the community.

# Picture glossary

**community** group of people living and working in the same area

**pet** animal that lives with people in their home

**zookeeper** person who works with wild animals in a zoo

# Index

# Notes for parents and teachers

This series introduces readers to the lives of different community workers, and explains some of the different jobs they perform around the world. Some of the locations featured include Zurich, Switzerland (page 4); New York City, USA (page 5); Washington, D.C., USA (page 6); Hangzhou, China (page 9); Ain Arab, Lebanon (page 18), and Ngamba Island (cover).

## Before reading
Talk to the children about the work of a vet. What do they think a vet does? Have they ever taken a pet to the vet's? Do they think vets only look after pets?

## After reading
• Set up the role play area as a vet's clinic. Use soft toys as "patients" and a table for examining the patients. Use a toy medical kit for assessing the patients. Ask the children what they think is wrong, and what they will do to make the pet better. Give children lengths of crepe bandage for wrapping round the sick pets.
• Play the game: "Who is coming to see the vet?" Say the rhyme: *Someone has come to see the vet. Is it a wild animal or a pet?* Then children should take it in turn to make the noise of the animal (A quack for a duck, a miaow for a cat etc.) and the "vet" has to guess what animal it is.
• Look through magazines and encourage children to cut out pictures of animals. Make a collage of these pictures and write at the top: *Vets help all these animals.*